COMPARING ANIMAL TRAITS

PLATYPUSES

WEB-FOOTED BILLED MAMMALS

REBECCA E. HIRSCH

Lerner Publications ◆ Minneapolis

Lerner Publications Company
A division of Lerner Publishing Group, Inc.
241 First Avenue North
Minneapolis, MN 55401 USA

For reading levels and more information, look up this title at www.lernerbooks.com.

Photo Acknowledgments

The images in this book are used with the permission of: © Roland Seitre/Minden Pictures/Newscom, pp. 1, 26 (left), 27 (right); © Shin Yoshino/Minden Pictures/Newscom, p. 4; © Dave Watts/Alamy, p. 5; © Robin Smith/Photographer's Choice/Getty Images, p. 6; © Jean-Paul Ferrero/ Auscape/Minden Pictures, p. 7 (top); © JTB MEDIA CREATION, Inc./Alamy, p. 7 (bottom); © iStockphoto.com/Leppert, p. 8 (right); © Ingo Schulz imageBROKER/Newscom, p. 8 (left); © Dave Watts/naturepl.com, p. 9 (left); © Jim Brandenburg/Minden Pictures/Newscom, p. 9 (right); © Christophe Courteau/naturepl.com, pp. 10, 11(top); © Clearviewimages RF/Alamy, p. 11 (bottom); © Mapping Specialists, Ltd., Madison, WI, p. 12; © Kevin Schafer/Oceans-Image/ Photoshot/Newscom, p. 13 (top); © Dave Watts/NHPA/Photoshot/Newscom, p. 13 (bottom); © K. Wothe/ picture alliance/Arco Images G/Newscom, p. 14; © Minden Pictures/SuperStock, p. 15 (top); © Arndt Sven-Erik/Arterra Picture Library/Alamy, p. 15 (bottom); © Suzi Eszterhas/Minden Pictures/Newscom, p. 16; © D. Parer & E. Parer-Cook/Minden Pictures/Newscom, p. 17 (left); © Ralph Lee Hopkins/National Geographic/ Getty Images, p. 17 (right); © Marie Read/Science Source, pp. 18, 23 (bottom); © blickwinkel/Alamy, p. 19; © Kike Calvo/Visual&Written SL/Alamy, p. 20; © Jason Edwards/National Geographic/Getty Images, p. 21 (left); © Flip Nicklin/Minden Pictures/Newscom, pp. 21 (right), 29 (bottom); © Stephen J. Krasemann/ Science Source, p. 22; © iStockphoto.com/michael_price, p. 23 (top); © Jason Edwards/National Geographic Stock, p. 24; © iStockphoto.com/JohnCarnemolla, p. 25; © iStockphoto.com/Shmenny50, p. 26 (right); © Jean-Philippe Varin/Science Source, p. 27 (left); © Phillip Colla/SeaPics.com, p. 28; © Mike Johnson/SeaPics.com, p. 29 (top).

Front cover: © Marie Read/Science Source.
Back cover: © worldswildlifewonders/Shutterstock.com.

Main body text set in Calvert MT Std 12/18. Typeface provided by Monotype Typography.

Library of Congress Cataloging-in-Publication Data

Hirsch, Rebecca E., author.
    Platypuses : web-footed billed mammals / by Rebecca E. Hirsch.
        pages   cm. — (Comparing animal traits)
    Includes index.
    ISBN: 978-1-4677-5581-8 (lib. bdg. : alk. paper)
    ISBN: 978-1-4677-6064-5 (pbk.)
    ISBN: 978-1-4677-6220-5 (EB pdf)
    1. Platypus—Behavior—Juvenile literature. 2. Platypus—Life cycles—Juvenile literature.
3. Platypus—Juvenile literature. I. Title.
QL737.M72H57 2015
599.2'9—dc23   2014020920

Manufactured in the United States of America
1 — BP —12/31/14

TABLE OF CONTENTS

MEET THE PLATYPUS

With a splash, a platypus dives into a river at night. It glides through the dark water, waving its bill from side to side in search of food. For a long time, the platypus puzzled scientists. What kind of animal was it? After years of study, scientists learned the answer. The platypus belongs to a group of animals called mammals. Other animal groups include insects, fish, amphibians, reptiles, and birds.

For many years, scientists were unsure whether the platypus fit into the mammal group.

All mammals share certain traits. Mammals are vertebrates—animals with backbones. They are warm-blooded. They have hair or fur on their bodies. Female mammals make milk for their babies. Platypuses have these traits. But they also have traits that make them unique.

Platypuses can easily swim through dark water.

CHAPTER 1

WHAT DO PLATYPUSES LOOK LIKE?

Platypuses love to dive and swim. Their flattened heads and webbed feet help them glide through water. Claws on platypuses' feet help them run on land. Thick, waterproof fur keeps platypuses warm and dry.

Platypuses have broad, flat tails. They use their tails for diving and steering underwater. The tail is also where the platypus stores its body fat. Platypuses use the stored fat for energy when food is scarce.

The flat tail of a platypus helps the mammal store energy and steer itself.

Male platypuses use venom-filled spurs to defend themselves from other animals.

The most unusual feature of a platypus is its bill. The black bill is soft and rubbery. Male platypuses have another odd feature: pointy **spurs** on their back ankles. Each spur is filled with **venom**. The male platypus defends itself with the spurs, jabbing **predators** and fighting other males during mating season. Bills and spurs are both rare among mammals.

DID YOU KNOW?

From the tip of its bill to the end of its tail, a platypus measures about 15 to 23 inches (38 to 60 centimeters) long. It weighs between 1.5 and 5 pounds (0.7 to 3 kilograms).

PLATYPUSES VS. BEAVERS

Beavers are furry, four-footed mammals. They live in rivers, lakes, and streams across North America, Europe, and Asia. Beavers are larger than platypuses. Even so, the two mammals have many traits in common.

Beavers and platypuses both have small eyes and ears, as well as layers of brown fur. Beavers' fur sheds water and keeps the animals dry. Like platypuses, beavers also have webbed feet and paddle-shaped tails. These body parts help them move through water. And like platypuses, beavers store body fat in their tails.

Beavers and platypuses both waddle when they walk, but they are strong swimmers. Like platypuses, beavers steer with their flat tails. When swimming, beavers glide slowly along the surface of the water. Onlookers can only see a beaver's back, the top of its head, and the flat tail that gives a beaver direction.

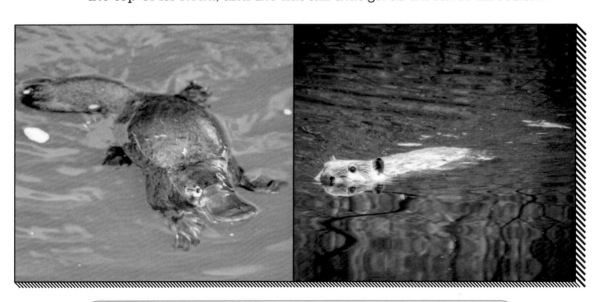

Platypuses and beavers both have bodies that are built for water travel.

COMPARE IT!

PLATYPUSES

VS.

BEAVERS

15 TO 23 INCHES (38 TO 60 CM)	◀ LENGTH ▶	**33 TO 49 INCHES** (84 TO 125 CM)
1.5 TO 5 POUNDS (0.7 TO 2.3 KG)	◀ WEIGHT ▶	**24 TO 66 POUNDS** (11 TO 30 KG)
Webbed front and back feet	◀ FEET ▶	Webbed back feet

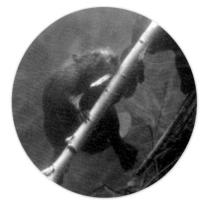

Double layer, waterproof ◀ FUR ▶ Double layer, waterproof

PLATYPUSES VS. GIRAFFES

Giraffes are the world's tallest mammals. They trot through woodlands, savannas, and grasslands in West Africa. They browse the tops of trees, filling up on leaves and buds. Giraffes are much bigger than platypuses. A grown giraffe is so tall that it can look over a treetop without having to stretch.

No other mammal stands as tall as a giraffe.

A giraffe's legs and neck are as long as an adult human is tall. Such long necks and legs allow giraffes to reach higher than other animals can reach. But a giraffe's height makes some activities a challenge. Unlike platypuses, whose short legs keep them close to the ground, giraffes have trouble bending low. A giraffe must spread its legs wide and bend its long neck to take a drink.

Giraffes can reach treetops more comfortably than they can drink from the ground.

Giraffes and platypuses both have fur. The platypus's thick fur helps it stay warm and dry. A giraffe's fur helps it hide from predators. The fur has a dark-and-light pattern. This pattern camouflages the giraffe in the spotted shade of trees.

DID YOU KNOW?
A giraffe's **TONGUE** is 18 inches (46 cm) long. That's about as long as a full-grown platypus!

CHAPTER 2

WHERE DO PLATYPUSES LIVE?

Platypuses are found in eastern Australia and on the nearby island of Tasmania. They inhabit lakes, streams, and rivers. The platypus's ideal habitat is a river with a rocky bottom, shady trees, and plenty of prey. These water-loving animals dive for insects, crayfish, shrimp, and other invertebrates.

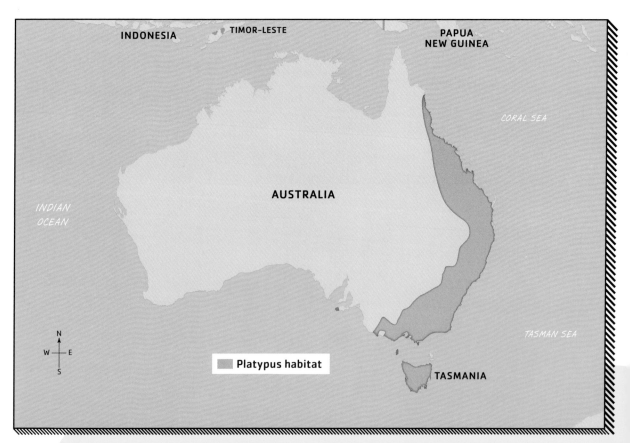

INDONESIA   TIMOR-LESTE

PAPUA
NEW GUINEA

CORAL SEA

AUSTRALIA

INDIAN
OCEAN

TASMAN SEA

N
W—E
S

Platypus habitat

TASMANIA

DID YOU KNOW?
In the past, people hunted platypuses for their **FUR**. The platypus population fell. In modern times, laws protect platypuses from hunters.

Platypuses dig burrows at a river's edge. Burrows give the platypus a safe place to rest. The burrows stay warm in winter and cool in summer. In wintertime, a platypus may stay inside its burrows for several days at a time.

Platypuses keep their burrows hidden. The entrance may be tucked under a bank or hidden in a tangle of weeds. This keeps platypuses safe from predators. Platypuses often dig several different burrows so that they have plenty of safe spots to hide.

The platypus's burrows help the animal stay hidden and secure.

PLATYPUSES VS. NORTH AMERICAN OTTERS

A North American otter slides headfirst down a muddy riverbank, moving toward the water. These mammals live in Canada and the United States. North American otters and platypuses have similar habitats. Both animals love rivers, streams, and lakes with trees nearby.

Like platypuses, North American otters hunt in freshwater. The otters live in lake and river habitats where food is plentiful. They love to eat fish. They will also eat crabs, crayfish, insects, and even birds.

Otters swim through rivers and lakes as they search for prey.

DID YOU KNOW?
People have hunted North American otters for their fur, as they once did platypuses. Some people **STILL DO**.

Platypuses build their living spaces. So do North American otters. An otter digs a burrow in the riverbank, as platypuses do. An otter may also move into a hollow log or a pile of driftwood. Like platypus burrows, the entrance of an otter den is hidden from predators. Otters enter their dens from underwater.

Like platypuses, otters live in dens.

PLATYPUSES VS. DALL SHEEP

Dall sheep are sure-footed mammals. They climb some of the steepest mountains in Alaska and Canada. Platypuses inhabit lakes and rivers. But Dall sheep are at home in high places.

Platypuses can find everything they need in one habitat. Dall sheep cannot. In summer, Dall sheep eat grasses, sedges, willows, and other plants that grow high in the mountains. In winter, these foods become scarce. Dall sheep must climb down the mountains. They seek out places where winds blow the snow away and expose plants underneath.

A Dall sheep's hoofs help the animal cling to cliffs and rocky ledges.

COMPARE IT!

PLATYPUSES	VS.	DALL SHEEP
STREAMS, RIVERS, AND LAKES	◄ HABITAT ►	MOUNTAINS
EASTERN AUSTRALIA	◄ GEOGRAPHIC RANGE ►	ALASKA AND NORTHWEST CANADA
insect larvae, crayfish, shrimp	◄ FOOD ►	grasses, sedges, shrubs

Dall sheep don't hide from predators the way platypuses do. They occupy open spaces with cliffs and rocky ledges nearby. They use their keen eyes to keep watch. If a sheep spots a gray wolf or a grizzly bear, it escapes to rocks and ledges where the predator can't follow.

CHAPTER 3

PLATYPUS HUNTING BEHAVIOR

Platypuses spend most of their time alone. During the day, these solitary mammals rest in burrows. At night, they head to the water to hunt. They dive for crayfish, shrimp, and other prey that live on the lake or the river bottom.

When the platypus dives, it closes its eyes, ears, and nose. So how does the platypus find food? It wiggles its bill. The bill can feel changes in water current. This lets the platypus know where to swim. Tiny cells in the bill can detect electricity given off by prey. This unusual ability is called electroreception.

A platypus starts its food search by wiggling its bill.

After catching a meal, a platypus heads back to the surface.

When the platypus locates prey, it digs in the rocks and mud. It scoops up its prey and stores the food in its cheeks. Then it paddles to the surface. Like all mammals, platypuses need air to breathe. At the surface of the water, the platypus treads water and chews its food. Platypuses have no teeth, yet they have no trouble chewing. They use small pads on their bills to grind their food.

PLATYPUSES VS. TUCUXI DOLPHINS

Tucuxi dolphins live in South America. You can find them in rivers and along coastlines. Tucuxi dolphins and platypuses have similar hunting behaviors. Both animals dive for prey on the bottom of the water. Both animals come to the surface to breathe.

Like platypuses, tucuxi dolphins cannot see their prey. They don't hunt in the dark, as platypuses do. But they do hunt in muddy waters. Tucuxi dolphins rely on echolocation. A dolphin makes clicking sounds and listens for an echo. The sound helps the dolphin find its way underwater. The sound also reveals where prey is located.

Tucuxi dolphins find prey by sensing electricity too. Platypuses and tucuxi dolphins are two of very few mammals known to have this ability. The platypus detects electricity with its bill. The tucuxi dolphin uses its snout. Tiny pits on the snout sense electrical currents. Then the dolphin locates the source of the current—a tasty fish.

Tucuxi dolphins breathe in oxygen and then dive underwater for prey.

COMPARE IT!

PLATYPUSES

TUCUXI DOLPHINS

	HUNTING GROUNDS	
RIVERS, STREAMS, AND LAKES		**RIVERS AND COASTLINES**

	HUNTING ADVANTAGE	
ELECTRORECEPTION		**ECHOLOCATION AND ELECTRORECEPTION**

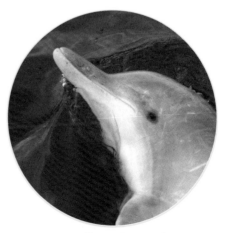

BILL ◀ ELECTRORECEPTION ORGAN ▶ **SNOUT**

PLATYPUSES VS. AFRICAN WILD DOGS

African wild dogs stalk game across grasslands, savannas, and open woodlands in Africa. Platypuses and African wild dogs are both predators, but they hunt in different ways. Unlike platypuses, African wild dogs hunt in groups. These mammals live in packs of six to twenty or more animals.

Cooperation is important among African wild dogs. They are smaller than prey animals such as zebras and antelope. By hunting together, African wild dogs can catch prey much larger than themselves. A pack of wild dogs can even bring down a 550–pound (250 kg) wildebeest.

African wild dogs work in groups to capture their meals.

Platypuses close their ears and eyes when hunting. But African wild dogs keep their ears and eyes open. As they spread out in search of prey, the dogs howl to keep track of group members. Their big ears can catch the sound from far away. When a dog spots prey with its sharp eyes, the pack approaches silently and then gives chase. African wild dogs can run for up to an hour while following prey.

An African wild dog's fur helps it stay hidden from prey.

DID YOU KNOW?
Platypuses **HUNT** alone and at night. But African wild dogs hunt during the day.

CHAPTER 4

THE LIFE CYCLE OF PLATYPUSES

Platypuses have an unusual life cycle. Female platypuses don't give birth to live young, as most female mammals do. Instead, platypuses lay eggs. After mating with a male platypus, a female platypus digs a burrow and builds a nest for her eggs. Platypuses lay one to three leathery eggs at a time.

Baby platypuses grow their fur coats within six weeks after their birth.

Juvenile platypuses typically start swimming around three months old.

The eggs hatch after ten days. Newborn platypuses don't look like their parents. The baby platypus is about the size of a kidney bean. It has no fur and can't see. The babies stay in the burrow and drink the mother's milk. By six weeks, the young platypuses are fully furred, can see, and can leave the burrow for short stretches. After four months, they begin to forage for food.

Platypuses are fully grown after eighteen months. Adult platypuses have inherited many traits from their parents. They have flat tails, webbed feet, and streamlined bodies for swimming. They can dig burrows. They use their bills to find food. With these traits, platypuses may survive for ten years or more.

PLATYPUSES VS. SHORT-BEAKED ECHIDNAS

Short-beaked echidnas live in Australia and New Guinea. You can find these spiny mammals in forests, meadows, and deserts. Like the platypus, the short-beaked echidna is one of the few egg-laying mammals. Short-beaked echidnas and platypuses also have similar life cycles.

The female echidna lays a single leathery egg. She stores the egg in a pouch on her belly. After ten days, the egg hatches. At first, the baby echidna—like a baby platypus—is tiny, blind, and hairless.

A baby echidna clings to hairs in its mother's pouch and drinks her milk. When the baby develops prickly spines, the mother removes it from her pouch. However, the young echidna continues drinking its mother's milk until it is six months old. Then it is ready to live on its own.

A baby echidna (*left*) develops spines as it grows into its adult state (*right*).

COMPARE IT!

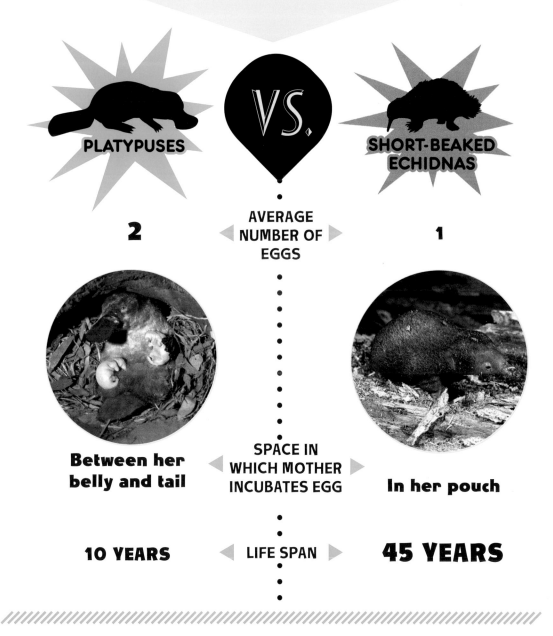

PLATYPUSES   VS.   **SHORT-BEAKED ECHIDNAS**

2   ◄ AVERAGE NUMBER OF EGGS ►   **1**

Between her belly and tail   ◄ SPACE IN WHICH MOTHER INCUBATES EGG ►   **In her pouch**

10 YEARS   ◄ LIFE SPAN ►   **45 YEARS**

Short-beaked echidnas reach adulthood at the same time as platypuses. They're **mature** at about eighteen months old. But short-beaked echidnas live longer than platypuses—as long as forty-five years.

PLATYPUSES VS. BLUE WHALES

Blue whales swim in all the oceans of the world. Like platypuses, these massive mammals are built for water travel. Unlike platypuses, they give birth to live young. A female blue whale has one calf every two to three years.

Blue whale calfs usually swim with their mothers nearby.

Young blue whales quickly begin to resemble their parents.

A newborn platypus is tiny, but a newborn blue whale is the largest infant mammal on Earth. It is longer and heavier than a pickup truck. When a baby platypus hatches, it is blind and helpless. But a newborn blue whale calf can swim right away. Even so, the mother swims close to her calf to keep it safe.

Female blue whales make milk for their babies, as all mammal mothers do. The babies nurse for as long as eight months—twice as long as baby platypuses. A blue whale calf can gain more than 200 pounds (91 kg) a day on its mother's rich milk. Platypuses live just ten years, but blue whales are some of the longest-lived animals on Earth. They can live for eighty or ninety years.

DID YOU KNOW?
A newborn blue whale weighs **5,000** to 6,000 pounds (2,267 to 2,721 kg) and stretches 25 feet (8 meters) long.

PLATYPUS TRAIT CHART

This book explored how platypuses are similar to and different from other mammals. What mammals would you add to this list?

	WARM-BLOODED	HAIR ON BODY	GIVES BIRTH TO LIVE YOUNG	WEBBED FEET	FRESHWATER HABITAT	SENSES ELECTRICITY
PLATYPUS	X	X		X	X	X
BEAVER	X	X	X	X	X	
GIRAFFE	X	X	X			
NORTH AMERICAN OTTER	X	X	X	X	X	
DALL SHEEP	X	X	X			
TUCUXI DOLPHIN	X	X	X		X	X
AFRICAN WILD DOG	X	X	X			
SHORT-BEAKED ECHIDNA	X	X				X
BLUE WHALE	X	X	X			

GLOSSARY

burrows: holes in the ground made by animals for shelter or protection

cells: any one of the very small parts that together form all living things

forage: to search for food

habitat: an environment where an animal naturally lives. A habitat is the place where an animal can find food, water, air, shelter, and a place to raise its young.

invertebrates: animals lacking a backbone. Insects, spiders, and worms are invertebrates.

mature: having reached adulthood

population: a group of one species of animal living in a particular area or habitat

predators: animals that hunt, or prey on, other animals

prey: an animal that is hunted and killed by a predator for food

savannas: grasslands containing scattered trees

sedges: marsh plants that look like grasses

solitary: living by itself. Solitary animals spend most of their time alone, except for mating and raising young.

spurs: stiff, pointed body parts

traits: features that are inherited from parents. Body size and fur color are examples of inherited traits.

venom: a harmful substance produced by an animal and passed to a victim, usually by biting or stinging

LERNER

SOURCE

Expand learning beyond the printed book. Download free, complementary educational resources for this book from our website, www.lerneresource.com.

SELECTED BIBLIOGRAPHY

"Animal Diversity Web." University of Michigan Museum of Zoology. April 10, 2014. http://animaldiversity.ummz.umich.edu/.

Macdonald, David. *The Encyclopedia of Mammals*. New York: Facts on File, 2001.

"Mammals." *Arkive*. April 22, 2014. http://www.arkive.org/mammals/.

"Mammals." Evolutionarily Distinct and Globally Endangered (EDGE). May 17, 2014. http://www.edgeofexistence.org/mammals/.

"Mammals." *National Geographic*. April 11, 2014. http://animals.nationalgeographic.com/animals/mammals/.

"Platypus, *Ornithorhynchus anatinus*." Parks and Wildlife Service, Tasmania. May 16, 2014. http://www.parks.tas.gov.au/index.aspx?base=4789.

"The Platypus: A Very Special Australian." Australian Platypus Conservancy. May 17, 2014. http://www.platypus.asn.au/.

FURTHER INFORMATION

Animal Fact Guide: Platypus
http://www.animalfactguide.com/animal-facts/platypus
Check out this site to find more facts about platypuses, as well as photos and a habitat map.

Arkive: Platypus
http://www.arkive.org/platypus/ornithorhynchus-anatinus
This site, from the wildlife group Wildscreen, features many photos, video, and audio clips of the platypus, as well as information about its biology and habitat.

Higgins, Nadia. *Deadly Adorable Animals*. Minneapolis: Lerner Publications, 2013. Learn more about platypuses and other cute but deadly animals.

Lunis, Natalie. *Electric Animals*. New York: Bearport, 2011. Pick up this book to discover the ways animals use electricity.

San Diego Zoo Animals: Mammals—Echidna
http://animals.sandiegozoo.org/animals/echidna
Visit this site from the San Diego Zoo to learn more about the platypus's spiky relative, the echidna.

INDEX